Bible Verse
Coloring Book

Prayer

This book belongs to:

_____

Praying always with all prayer and supplication in the Spirit, and watching thereunto with all perseverance and supplication for all saints;

Ephesians 6:18

[The righteous] cry, and the LORD heareth, and delivereth them out of all their troubles.

Psalms 34:17

And he spake a parable unto them [to this end], that men ought always to pray, and not to faint;

Luke 18:1

After this manner therefore pray ye: Our Father which art in heaven, Hallowed be thy name.

Matthew 6:9

Then shall ye call upon me, and ye shall go and pray unto me, and I will hearken unto you.

Jeremiah 29:12

Continue in prayer, and watch in the same with thanksgiving.

Colossians 4:2

Rejoicing in hope; patient in tribulation; continuing instant in prayer.

Romans 12:12

The Lord is nigh unto all them that call upon him, to all that call upon him in truth.

Psalm 145:18

For where two or three are gathered together in my name, there am I in the midst of them.

Matthew 18:20

Let us therefore come boldly unto the throne of grace, that we may obtain mercy, and find grace to help in time of need.

Hebrews 4:16

And at midnight Paul and Silas prayed, and sang praises unto God: and the prisoners heard them.

Acts 16:25

And if we know
that he hear us,
whatsoever we ask,
we know that
we have the
petitions that we
desired of him.

1 John 5:15

But let him ask in faith, nothing wavering. For he that wavereth is like a wave of the sea driven with the wind and tossed.

James 1:6

But the end
of all things
is at hand: be ye
therefore sober,
and watch
unto prayer.

1 Peter 4:7

And whatsoever ye shall ask in my name, that will I do, that the Father may be glorified in the Son.

John 14:13

Be careful for nothing; but in every thing by prayer and supplication with thanksgiving let your requests be made known unto

Philippians 4:6

If ye abide in me, and my words abide in you, ye shall ask what ye will, and it shall be done unto you.

John 15:7

Therefore I say unto you, What things soever ye desire, when ye pray, believe that ye receive [them], and ye shall have [them].

Mark 11:24

Pray without ceasing.

1 Thessalonians 5:17

But thou, when thou prayest, enter into thy closet, and when thou hast shut thy door, pray to thy Father which is in secret; and thy Father which seeth in secret shall reward thee openly.

Matthew 6:6

And I say unto you,
Ask, and it shall
be given you;
seek, and ye
shall find;
knock, and it shall
be opened
unto you.

Luke 11:9

I exhort therefore, that, first of all, supplications, prayers, intercessions, [and] giving of thanks, be made for all men;

1 Timothy 2:1

Call unto me,
and I will answer
thee, and shew
thee great and
mighty things,
which thou
knowest not.

Jeremiah 33:3

Watch and pray, that ye enter not into temptation: the spirit indeed [is] willing, but the flesh [is] weak.

Matthew 26:41

Confess [your] faults one to another, and pray one for another, that ye may be healed. The effectual fervent prayer of a righteous man availeth much.

James 5:16

Made in the USA
Las Vegas, NV
25 September 2021